These jokes may be hazardous to your bad mood. Read with caution.

Author: The Editors at Tangerine Press

Copyright ° 2005 Scholastic Inc

Scholastic and Tangerine Press and associated logos
are trademarks of Scholastic Inc

Published by Tangerine Press,
an imprint of Scholastic Inc.,
557 Broadway, New York, NY 10012

10 9 8 7 6 5 4 3 2 1

ISBN: 0-439-74382-6

Printed and bound in Canada

tangerine
press
an imprint of
SCHOLASTIC
www.scholastic.com

Funny Farm

Why do ducks have flat feet?
To stamp out forest fires.
Why do elephants have flat feet?
To stamp out burning ducks.

Why did the rabbit cross the road?
To get to the hopping mall.

What do you call a chicken that crosses the road without looking both ways?
Dead.

Why did the hen go halfway across the road and stop?
She wanted to lay it on the line.

Why did the sheep cross the road?
He needed to go to the baa baa shop.

3

**How do you stop a bull
from charging?**

Take away his credit cards.

**Why did the turkey cross
the road?**

It was the chicken's day off.

**What do you call a bunch
of ducks in a crate?**

A box of quackers.

**Why did the duck cross
the road?**

*Because the chicken retired
and moved to Florida.*

Why did the chicken cross the playground?

To get to the other slide.

Why did the goose cross the road?

The police officer waved him across.

What was the farmer doing across the road?

Trying to catch all of his chickens.

Did you hear the one about the peacock that crossed the road?

It's a really colorful tail.

Why did Bo Peep lose her sheep?

She had a crook with her.

What do you get if you cross a chicken with a cement mixer?

A brick-layer!

How do you fit more pigs on your farm?

Build a sty-scraper.

Why does a rooster watch TV?

For hentertainment.

What do you call a cow in Alaska?

An Eskimoo.

What kind of doctor treats ducks?

A quack!

Why did the chicken cross the road?

To prove he wasn't chicken.

Why did the chicken cross the Internet?

To get to the other site.

**Why did the rooster
run away?**
He was chicken.

**Why is it easy for
chicks to talk?**
Because talk is cheep.

**What do you call a rooster
that wakes up at the same
time every morning?**
An alarm cluck.

**What do you get if you
cross a cow with a camel?**
Lumpy milkshakes.

What is the definition of a goose?
*An animal that grows down as it
grows up.*

**What animal goes to bed
with his shoes on?**

A horse.

**What do you give a
pony with a cold?**

Cough stirrup.

**What happens to a flock of
geese that land in a volcano?**

Their goose is cooked.

**What is a horse's
favorite sport?**

Stable tennis.

**What do you give
a sick pig?**

Oinkment.

Who was the meanest chicken?

Attila the Hen.

**What do teenage geese
worry about?**

Getting goose pimples.

**What did the farmer call
the cow that would not give
him any milk?**

An udder failure.

What is a pig's favorite ballet?

Swine Lake.

**What's the best way to keep
milk from turning sour?**

Leave it in the cow.

**How do you stop a rooster
from crowing on Sunday?**

Eat him on Saturday.

Where do milkshakes come from?

Excited cows!

**What is the opposite of
cock-a-doodle-doo?**

Cock-a-doodle-don't.

What would happen if bulls could fly?
*Beef would go up and you'd have to carry
an umbrella with you all the time.*

**What do you get if your farm
animals walk under the clouds?**
They'll be under the weather.

**What goes "peck, bang, peck,
bang, peck, bang?"**
*A bunch of chickens in a field full
of balloons.*

**How do you get a pig
to the hospital?**
By Hambulance.

**What do you call a jokebook
for chickens?**
A yolk book.

Who tells chicken jokes?
Comedihens!

**What did the lovesick bull
say to the cow?**
*"When I fall in love it will be
for heifer."*

**What do you call a sheep
with no head or legs?**
A cloud!

**What do you get if you feed
dynamite to a chicken?**
An egg-splosion!

**What do you call a chicken
in a shellsuit?**

An egg.

**What do you call a pig that
drives dangerously?**

A road hog.

**What does a farmer say
to his cows as he's milking
them?**

Udder nonsense.

**What is the easiest way to
count a herd of cattle?**

Use a cowculator.

**What is a cows favorite
vegetable?**

A cowat.

What did the baby chick say when he saw his mother sitting on an orange?

"Dad, Dad, look what marma-laid!"

What do you get when a chicken lays an egg on top of a barn?

An eggroll.

What do you get if you cross a chicken with a duck?

A chicken that lays down.

Why does a chicken coop have two doors?
Because if it had four doors it would be a sedan.

What do you call the story of the *Three Little Pigs*?
A Pigtail.

Where do cows go on Saturday night?
To the moo-vies!

Why did the turkey inhale his food?
Because he was a gobbler.

Who is the most famous celebrity chicken?
Gregory Peck.

**What is another name
for a cow?**

A lawn moo-er.

**Is chicken soup good
for your health?**

Not if you're a chicken.

Why did the chicken cross the road?

To prove to the possum it could be done.

Why didn't the chicken's skeleton cross the road?
He didn't have enough guts.

What do you call a pig thief?
A hamburglar.

How do sheep stay warm in winter?
They have central bleating.

How do chickens dance?
Chick to chick.

What do you call a bull who tells jokes?
Laugh-a-bull!

What dance will a chicken not do?

The foxtrot.

What is a duck's favorite dance?

The quackstep.

What do you get if you cross a cow, a sheep, and a goat?

A milky, baa kid.

What do you call a sleeping bull?

A bulldozer.

What game to cows play at parties?

Moosical chairs!

Why did Beethoven get rid of his chickens?

Because all they would say is BACH, BACH, BACH!

What do you call a horse that comes out only on Halloween?

A night-mare!

Where does a sheep go to get a haircut?

To the baa-baa shop.

What did the cow say to her calf about his messy room?

Where were you raised, a barn?

What famous beach do cows go to for vacation?

Moooiami Beach!

What is a cow's favorite city?

Moo York City.

What do you get when you cross a chicken with a dinosaur?

Tyrannosaurus Pecks.

What do calves go for lunch?

To the calf-ateria!

What do you call a duck wearing a hat?

A duck.

Why did the turkey cross the road?

To prove he wasn't chicken!

A duck walked into a store and asked, "Do you have any grapes?" The owner says, "No." The duck asks him three more times if he has any grapes. The owner said "NO, and if you ask me again, I'll nail your feet to the floor." The duck asked, "Do you have any nails?" The owner said, "No." So the duck asked, "Do you have any grapes?"

What do you call a pig that knows karate?
A porkchop.

What is the best way to stuff a turkey?
Take him to an all-you-can-eat buffet.

What is the hardest thing about riding a horse?
The ground!

**What is smarter than
a talking horse?**

A spelling bee.

**What did the duck say when
it laid a square egg?**

Ouch!

**What kind of horse can
swim underwater?**

A seahorse.

**What do cows like
to dance to?**

Any kind of moosic!

**What do you give a pony
with a cold?**

Cough Stirrup!

What do you get if a farm animal walks under a cloud?

An animal that is under the weather.

What do you get if you cross a chicken with a cement mixer?

A brick-layer.

Why does a rooster watch TV?

For hentertainment.

What goes "oom, oom?"

A cow walking backwards.

Why did the cow jump over the moon?

Because the farmer's hands were cold!

**What do you get if you
cross a hen with a dog?**

Pooched eggs.

**Why did the ram fall
over the cliff?**

He didn't see the ewe turn.

**What bird steals the soap
from the bathtub?**

A robber duck.

**What happens when a duck
flies upside-down?**

It quacks up.

**What do you call
a crazy chicken?**

A cuckoo cluck!

**What do you call a
dancing sheep?**
A baa-lerina.

**What do you call a sheep
that is very quiet?**
Asleep.

**What do you get if you cross
a sheep and a porcupine?**
*An animal that can knit its
own sweater.*

**What do you call a cow
lying on the ground?**
Ground beef.

**What do you call a cow
with only two legs?**
Lean beef!

What do you call a cow that has just given birth?

Decalf-inated.

What do you call a cow with a twitch?

Beef jerky.

What do you call a place full of ancient cows?

A mooseum.

What do you get from old cows?

Wrinkle cream.

What do you get when you cross a cow and a ghost?

Vanishing cream!

What does a cow call a fly?
A moo-sance.

**What is a cow's
favorite drink?**
Lemoooonade.

**What kind of car does
a cow drive?**
A cattle-ac.

**What restaurant did the
cow like to visit?**
Dairy Queen.

Where do cows buy gifts?
From a cattle-og!

Why can't you tell a cow a secret?
Because it goes in one ear and out the udder.

Why did the farmer buy a brown cow?
He wanted chocolate milk.

Why do cows have bells?
Because their horns don't work.

How do pigs write top secret messages?
With a pig pen filled with invisible oink.

Why should you never tell a secret to a pig?
Because they love to squeal!

Where do horses shop?
Old Neigh-vy!

**Why did the horse eat
with its mouth open?**
*Because he had bad
stable manners.*

**Where did the duck go
when he was sick?**
To the ducktor.

**What did the duck say
to the waitress?**
Put it on my bill!

**What do you call a duck
with fangs?**
Count Duckula.

What do ducks have with soup?
Quakers.

What do ducks watch on TV?
Duck-umentaries.

What time does a duck wake up?
At the quack of dawn.

Two cows were talking in a field. One said to the other, "What do you think of this mad cow disease?" The other cow replied, "I'm not worried. It doesn't affect us ducks."

Zany Zoo

Why do elephants paint themselves yellow?

To hide in a bowl of banana pudding.

Have you ever seen an elephant in a bowl of banana pudding?

Then it must work.

How can you get a bunch of elephants to get into a small yellow car?

Tell them it's banana pudding.

How can you know that an elephant has been in your fridge?

There are elephant prints in the butter.

Why did the elephant cross the road?

He was playing tag with the chicken!

33

**Why did the one handed
gorilla cross the road?**

*To get to the
secondhand shop.*

**Why did the otter
cross the road?**

To get to the otter side.

**What do you call a tiger
at the beach?**

Sandyclaws.

**Why did the monkey fall
from the tree?**

He let go.

**Why do mother kangaroos
hate rainy days?**

*Because the kids have
to play inside!*

What's black and white and has wheels?

A Giant Panda on rollerskates.

What do llamas like to eat?

Llama beans.

What do you cook on in the jungle?

A gorilla. Get it...grill-a!

What shouldn't you play cards with a big cat?

Because he's a cheetah.

Why are monkeys so noisy?

Because they were raised in the zoo.

Why did the baby bear join the Boy Scouts?

He wanted to be a cub scout.

Why can't the bears get into the house?

Goldi locked the door.

What do you call a bear with no ear?

A "B".

36

What is black and white with red polka dots?

A zebra with chicken pox.

Where does a 400-pound gorilla sit?

Anywhere he wants.

What is as big as an elephant but weighs nothing?

The elephant's shadow.

What did the otter say about the oil spill?

I otter get outta here.

What is black and white, black and white, black and white, and green?

Three zebras fighting over a pickle!

Why did the elephant lie on his back with his feet in the air?

To trip birds.

What time is it when an elephant sits on the park bench?

Time to get a new bench.

Why do giraffes have such long legs?

Because they have very smelly feet.

What do you get when you cross a rhinoceros with a black bird?

A lot of broken telephone wires.

How do you fix a broken chimp?

With a monkey wrench!

Where do baby apes sleep?

In ape-ri-cots.

**Why did the giant ape climb
the skyscraper?**

The elevator was broken.

**What is the difference between
an elephant and a flea?**

*An elephant can have fleas, but a
flea can't have elephants.*

**Why did the elephant paint
his toenails red?**

*So he could hide in
a cherry tree.*

**How do you know when an
elephant is under your bed?**

*When your nose touches the
ceiling!*

What do you call an elephant that flies fast?

A Dumbo jet.

What do you get when you cross an elephant with a kangaroo?

Big holes all over Australia.

How does an elephant get out of a tree?

He sits on a leaf and waits until autumn.

What do you get when an elephant skydives?

A big hole.

How do you get six elephants into a matchbox?

First, you take out the matches.

How does an elephant get out of a small car?

The same way he got in.

What kind of animal do you look like when you get out of the tub?

A little bear.

Why would you take a bear to the zoo?

Because he'd rather go to the movies!

What is a bear's favorite drink?
Coka Koala.

Why did the elephant paint himself different colors?
So he could hide in a box of crayons.

Why were the elephants thrown out of the pool?
They couldn't keep their trunks up.

Why did the elephant wear sneakers?
So he could sneak up on a mouse.

What kind of bears like to go out in the rain?
Drizzly bears!

What do you call an elephant at the North Pole?

Lost!

What does the lion say to his friends before a hunt?

Let us prey.

What did the lion say to the cub when he taught him to hunt?

Don't cross the road until you see the chicken.

What is a lion's favorite meal?

Baked beings.

What do tigers wear to bed?

Striped pajamas.

What happened when the lion ate the comedian?

He felt funny!

What is striped and bouncy?

A tiger on a pogostick.

How can you get a set of teeth put in for free?

Tease a lion.

How does a cheetah greet other animals on the savanna?

Pleased to eat you.

What do you get if you cross a cheetah with a sheep?

A spotted sweater.

What is the difference between a lion and a tiger?

A tiger has the mane part missing!

What happened to the leopard who took a bath three times a day?

He was spotless.

What do you get if you cross a lion with a snowman?

Frostbite.

What do you get if you cross a tiger with a kangaroo?

A striped jumper.

How are tigers like army sergeants?

They both have stripes.

What do you get if you cross a leopard with a watchdog?

A terrified policeman!

Lions eat people on what day?

Chewsday.

What did the lioness say to her cub while he was hunting?

Stop playing with your food.

What do you call a lion with a flower in his mane?

A dandy lion.

What do you get if you cross a lion with a train?

The end of the lion.

What do you call a show full of lions?

The mane event!

**How does a leopard
change its spots?**

*He gets up and moves
to another spot.*

**What happened to the man
that tried to cross a lion
with a goat?**

He had to get a new goat.

**Why did the lion tamer
get a ticket?**

He crossed the yellow lion.

**What do tigers sing
at Christmas?**

Jungle bells, jungle bells.

**What is the fiercist flower
in the garden?**

A tiger lily!

**Why did the lion spit out
the clown?**

Because he tasted funny.

**What should you know if you
want to be a lion tamer?**

More than the lion.

**What is the difference
between a dark sky and a lion?**

One pours rain, the other roars in pain.

**Who went into the tiger's
den and came out alive?**

The tiger.

**Why do cheetahs eat
raw meat?**

Because they can't cook.

What do you call a lion who has eaten your mother's sister?

An aunt eater.

What was the name of the scary movie about the killer lion?

Claws.

If a four-legged animal is a quadruped, and a two-legged creature is a biped, what is a tiger?

A stri-ped.

What do you call a flying primate?

A hot air baboon.

What do you call a naughty monkey?

A Badboon!

What do you call an exploding monkey?

A baBOOM!

What is a monkey's favorite cookie?

Chocolate chimp.

What is the first thing a monkey learns in school?

His Ape, B, Cs.

When do monkeys fall from the sky?

During Ape-ril showers.

Which sea will make you go ape?

The chimpan-sea!

52

How do elephants talk to each other?

On the elephone.

What do you call a sick elephant?

An ill-ephant.

What do you get if you cross a fish with an elephant?

Swimming trunks.

What did the grape do when the elephant sat on it?

It let out a little wine.

What's blue and has big ears?

An elephant at the North Pole!

Pets on Parade

What is gray, has big ears, and a trunk?

A mouse going on vacation.

What is a mouse's favorite game?

Hide and squeak.

What has 12 feet, 6 eyes, 3 tails, and can't see?

Three blind mice.

What squeaks when it solves a crime?

Miami Mice.

What do you get if you put some mice in the freezer?

Mice cubes!

**How do you keep a dog
from crossing the street?**
Put him in a barking lot.

**What did the canary say
when its cage fell apart?**
Cheep, cheep.

**If there are ten cats in
a boat and one jumps off,
how many are left?**
None, because the rest are copycats.

**What is a cat's
favorite color?**
Purrrple.

**What do you call Christopher
Columbus's cat?**
Christofurry Columbus!

**What do cats eat
for breakfast?**

Mice Krispies.

**When is it a bad time to
cross a black cat?**

When you're a mouse.

**What did the female cat say
to the male cat?**

You're the purrfect cat for me.

**What do you get when you
cross a cat with a parrot?**

A carrot.

**What do you call a hamster that
can pick up an elephant?**

Sir!

How do you stop a dog from barking in the backyard?
Put him in the front yard.

What do you say to a dog before he eats?
Bone appetite.

How do you find a lost dog?
Put your ear to a tree and listen for the bark.

What word can a dog say?
Bark.

What is small, furry, and smells like bacon?
A hamster!

What is small, has a long tail, and works for the police?

A gerbil shepherd.

What is a duck's favorite dance?

The quackstep.

When should a mouse carry an umbrella?

When it's raining cats and dogs.

What is small, furry, and a great swordfighter?

A mouseketeer.

What is gray, hairy, and lives on a man's face?

A mouse-tache!

What is gray and furry on the inside, and white on the outside?

A mouse sandwich.

What is a duck's favorite dance?

The quackstep.

How do mice celebrate when they move into a new home?

With a mouse warming party.

What did the mouse say when he broke his front teeth?

That was hard cheese!

What is the definition of a narrow squeak?

A thin mouse.

What goes dot, dot, squeak?

Mouse code.

What do get if you cross a mouse with laundry detergent?

Squeaky clean.

What goes eek, eek, BANG?

A mouse in a minefield!

What is squeaky and hangs around in caves?

Stalagmice.

What mouse was a Roman emperor?

Julius Cheeser.

Who was the most powerful mouse in China?

Mouse Tse Tung.

**Hickory Dickory dock.
The mouse ran up the clock.
The clock struck one,
but the rest got away with
minor injuries.**

**What kind of dog loves
to take a bubble bath?**
A shampoodle!

**What kind of dog does
a vampire have?**
A bloodhound.

**What dogs are best for
sending telegrams?**
Wire-haired terriers.

**What do call a crazy dog
from Australia?**
A dingo-ling.

**What is a small dog's
favorite city?**
New Yorkie!

How do dogs do when they have to go to the bathroom during a movie?

They hit the paws button!

Why can't Dalmatians hide?

They are always spotted.

How do you stop a dog from digging in your garden?

Take away his shovel.

What did the dog get when he graduated from school?

A pedigree.

What do you call a dog in the library?

A hush puppy!

What do you get when you cross a dog with a phone?

A golden receiver!

What do you get when you cross a mean dog with a computer?

A mega-bite.

What does a lazy dog chase?

Parked cars.

What dog always knows what time it is?

A watch dog.

What is a dog's favorite pizza?

Pupperoni!

Silly Snakes
and other comical creatures

What is a snake's favorite subject?

Hiss-tory!

What kind of snake is good at math?

An adder.

What do you give a sick snake?

Asp-rin.

What do you get if you cross a snake with a Lego set?

A boa constructor.

Why do babies like snakes?

Some come with their own rattle!

What do snakes write at the bottom of their letters?

With love and hisses!

What do you get if you cross a snake and a pig?

A boar constrictor.

Which hand would you use to pick up a snake?

Someone else's.

What do you do if you find a poisonous snake in the bathroom?

Wait until he's done.

What do you get if you cross a snake and a trumpet?

A snake in the brass!

What do you call a snake that thinks he's a bird?

A feather boa!

What is a snake's favorite dance?

Snake, rattle and roll.

What is a snake's second favorite dance?

The Mamba.

**What do you get when you
cross a snake with a hotdog?**
A fangfurter!

**Why did the two boa constrictors
get married?**
*Because they had a crush
on each other.*

Why are snakes hard to fool?
They have no legs to pull.

**What kind of snake is useful
on your windshield?**
A viper.

What perfume do snakes like?
Poison© by Christian Dior!

**What do you call a python with
a great bedside manner?**

A snake charmer!

**What do most people do
when they see a snake?**

They re-coil.

**What do snakes have on
their bathroom towels?**

Hiss and Hers.

**What do you get if you cross two
snakes with a magic spell?**

Addercadabra and abradacobra.

**What did the mother snake
say to her baby with a cold?**

Viper your nose!

What is a snake's favorite plant?
Poison ivy!

**What is the best thing
about a deadly snake?**
It has poisonality.

**Where do lizards go when
they lose their tails?**
To a retail shop.

**What is long, green,
and goes hith?**
A snake with a lisp.

Why did the wasp cross the road?
To get to the waspital!

What do you call a snake that works for the government?

A civil serpent.

What do you get when you cross a snake and kangaroo?

A jumprope!

Jumpin' Jokes

What's green and red?
A very mad frog!

What is green with red spots?
A frog with chicken pox.

What kind of shoes do frogs wear?
Open toad sandals.

How does a frog feel when he's sick?
Unhoppy.

Why did the frog read Sherlock Holmes?
He likes a good croak and dagger story!

What happened to the frog's car when the parking meter expired?

It got toad!

What is green, green, green, and green?

A frog rolling down hill.

What is a frog's favorite time?

Leap Year.

Why did the frog cross the road?

He wanted to jump to the other pond.

Why did the frog cross the road?

It was stuck to the chicken!

How do you confuse a frog?
Put it in a round pond and tell it to swim to the corner!

How does a frog confuse you?
He gets out of the pond, and says the corner of the pond is perfect for his new home.

What did the frog say to the fly?
You're really starting to bug me.

What does a frog say when it sees something cool?
Toadally awesome.

What do you call a frog with no legs?
It doesn't matter! He won't come anyway!

What are a frog's legs called?
Dinner!

Why did the frog croak?
Because the fly was poisoned.

**What did the frog order
from McDonald's?**
An order of flies and a diet croak.

**What is a frog's
favorite game?**
Croaket.

**Why did the frog go to the
hospital?**
It needed a hopperation!

What is black, white, and green?
A frog sitting on a newspaper!

Why should you never give a frog a newspaper?
He'll rip-it!

What is green and red, and goes 175 mph?
A frog in a blender!

**What is the thirstiest frog
in the world?**

The one that drank Canada Dry!

**What do fashion fab
frogs wear?**

Jumpsuits.

**What has more lives
than a cat?**

A frog. He croaks every night!

**Why did the frog go
to the bank?**

To robbit!

Why are frogs such liars?

Because they are am-FIB-ians!

**What did the frog do after
it heard a funny joke?**

It started to croak up!

**What do you get if you cross a steer
with a tadpole?**

A bullfrog.

**Why did the frogs cross
the road?**

To get a croak-a-cola.

**What did the frog say
at the library?**

Read it! Read it! Read it!

**What does a frog do after
he washes the car?**

Rub it, Rub it, Rub it!

Wacky Woods

Why did the wasp cross the road?

It had to go to waspital!

Why do skunks argue when crossing the road?

Because they like to raise a stink.

Why did the turtle cross the road?

To get to the shell station.

What kind of bird does construction work?

A crane.

Why did the judge say when he saw the skunk in the courtroom?

Odor in the court!

What is worse than a centipede with sore feet?

A giraffe with a sore throat.

What is black and white, black and white, black and white?

A skunk rolling down a hill.

What is black and white, black and white, black and white, and red?

Three skunks fighting over a tomato.

Why did the deer cross the freeway?

I don't know. He didn't live to tell the joke.

Why do you call a deer with no eyes?

No I-deer!

What is a twip?

A twip is what a wabbit takes when he wides on a twain.

How do you catch a squirrel?

Climb a tree and act like a nut.

How do you stop a skunk from smelling?

Hold its nose.

Where does a bee go to the bathroom?

At a BP station.

Why was the knight afraid of a bug?

Because it was a dragonfly.

**Why don't seagulls fly
over the bay?**

Because then they would be bagels.

**What kind of suit does
a bee wear to work?**

A buzzness suit.

**Why do birds fly south for
the winter?**

Because its too far to walk.

**Why did the man throw his
buttered toast?**

He wanted to watch the butterfly.

**What is the biggest ant
in the world?**

A giant!

What do you call a skunk that flies?

A smellicopter.

Why don't deer have uncles?

Because they only have antlers.

What is the best kind of computer bug?

Spiders ... they have the best web sites.

How do you catch a unique rabbit?

Unique up on him.

How to do catch a tame rabbit?

The tame way!

How do you milk an ant?
First you get a very small stool...

**What do porcupines say
when they kiss?**
Ouch!

Why do bears have fur coats?
Because they'd look stupid in a parka.

**Why did the rabbit go to
the doctor?**
Because he felt jumpy.

**What jumps up and down in
front of a car?**
Froglights.

What do you get if you cross a dog with a frog?

A croaker spaniel!

Where do frogs keep their money?

In a river bank.

What do you call a frog who wants to be a cowboy?

Hoppalong Cassidy.

What does a reindeer say before telling a joke?

This one will sleigh you!

Why did the reindeer wear red boots?

Because his black ones were muddy.

How long should a reindeer's legs be?

Long enough to reach the ground.

Why did the deer wear sunglasses?

He didn't want to be recognized.

What kind of deer has the shortest legs?

The smallest one.

Where do you find reindeer?

I depends on where you left them!

**What do porcupines have
that no other animal has?**

Baby porcupines.

**How many legs does
a deer have?**

*Six. Forelegs in the front
and two in the back.*

**What is the difference between
a skunk and a cookie?**

*You wouldn't want to dunk
a skunk in milk.*

**Why do rabbits scratch
themselves?**

*Because they are the only ones
who know where they itch.*

What is the wettest animal?
A rain-deer!

**What kind of math
do owls like?**
Owlgebra.

**What do you call a bee that
can't make up his mind?**
A maybee.

**How can you make a tarantula
shake?**
Run up behind it and yell, "BOO!"

**Which bug gobbles up
trash?**
The litterbug.

Why do you call spiders that just got married?

Newlywebs.

What is green and slimy, and found at the North Pole?

A very lost frog.

What is a frog's favorite candy?

Lollihops.

How do you know carrots are good for the eyes?

Have you ever seen a rabbit wearing glasses?

What did the rabbit give his girlfriend?

A 14-carrot ring.

What did the rabbits do after their wedding?

They went on a bunnymoon.

What do you get when you cross a rabbit with a leaf blower?

A hare dryer!

What is a rabbit's favorite music?

Hip-Hop.

What is white and has long ears, whiskers, and sixteen wheels?

Two rabbits on rollerskates.

What is a rabbit's favorite game?

Hopscotch.

**What's the name of the rabbit
that stole from the rich and
gave to the poor?**
Rabbit Hood.

**Why did the bunny build
herself a new house?**
She was tired of the hole thing.

**What did the bunny
say to the duck?**
You quack me up.

**Did you hear the joke
the duck told the
skunk?**
*You don't want to;
it really stinks.*

**Why don't rabbits get hot
in the summertime?**

They have hare conditioning.

**What did the bird say to
the losing army?**

Re-tweet!

**What do you call
a sick eagle?**

Ill-eagle.

**What bird is good
at making bread?**

A dough dough.

**What do you get if you cross
a lawn mower and a canary?**

Shredded tweet.

What do you give a sick bird?

The tweetment.

**What is a bird's
favorite cookie?**

Chocolate chirp.

**What kind of birds
stick together?**

Vel-crows!

**What is the difference
between a fly and a bird?**

*A bird can fly, but a
fly can't bird.*

**When does a teacher
carry birdseed?**

*When there is a
parrot-teacher conference.*

**When is the best time
to buy a canary?**

When they're going "cheep."

**What bird is with you
at every meal?**

A swallow.

**What is the best way to
catch a rabbit?**

*Hide in the brush and make a
sound like a lettuce.*

**What is white and has long ears,
whiskers, and sixteen wheels?**

Two rabbits on rollerskates.

**What do vultures always
have for dinner?**

Leftovers.

What is smaller than an ant's dinner?

An ant's mouth.

Who was the most famous ant scientist?

Albert Antstein

What game do ants play with elephants?

Squash.

What is the definition of a caterpillar?

A worm in a fur coat.

What is a mosquito's favorite sport?

Skin diving.

Underwater Jokes

Did you hear about the Broadway musical about sardines?

It's really packing them in.

What did Cinderella fish wear to the ball?

Glass flippers.

What do you call a big fish who makes you an offer you can't refuse?

The Codfather.

What kind of fish can perform an operation?

A sturgeon.

What happened to the shark that swallowed some keys?

He got lock jaw.

Where do fish wash?

In a river basin.

Why did the whale cross the ocean?

To get to the other tide.

Where do little fish go every morning?

To school.

What kind of fish moves up river at 100 mph?

A motor pike!

What do you get from a mean shark?

As far away as possible.

**What do sardines call
a submarine?**

A can of people.

**What is the difference between
a fish and a piano?**

*You can't tuna fish, but you can
tune a piano.*

Why are sardines not so bright?

*They end up in a can with a closed lid,
and leave the key outside.*

**What's the coldest animal
in the sea?**

A blue whale.

**Where do you find an
octopus that is at the
end of its rope?**

On squid row.

What kind of fish helps you hear better?

A herring aid.

What do you call a fish with no eyes?

Fsh.

How do fish go into business?

They start on a small scale.

What lives in the ocean, is grouchy, and hates the neighbors?

A hermit crab.

What kind of fish only swims at night?

A starfish.

**What kind of fish go to heaven
when they die?**

Angelfish.

**What kind of money do
fishermen make?**

Net profits.

**What kind of fish goes well
with peanut butter?**

Jellyfish.

What game do fish like to play?

Name that Tuna!

**What do you get if you
cross a big fish with
electricity?**

An electric shark.

**What is a dolphin's favorite
TV show?**
Whale of Fortune.

**Why are fish boots the
warmest to wear?**
Because they have electric eels.

**Why are dolphins smarter
than humans?**
*Within 3 hours, they can train a man to stand
by the side of a pool and feed them fish.*

**Where do fish go to
borrow money?**
A loan shark.

Why are goldfish orange?
The water makes them rusty.

Who held the baby octopus for ransom?

Squidnappers.

What was the Csar of Russia's favorite fish?

Csardines!

How do fish get to school?

By octobus.

Why did the fish blush?
Because the sea weed.

**What part of a fish
weighs the most?**
It's scales.

**What is dry on the outside,
filled with water, and can
blow up buildings?**
A fish tank.

**Who sits at the bottom of the
western sea?**
Clamity Jane.

**Where does seaweed look
for a job?**
In the "Kelp wanted" section.

What kind of fish is helpful to have in the winter?

A skate.

What kind of sharks never eat women?

Man eating sharks.

What is the best way to communicate with a fish?

Drop it a line.

How do you weigh a whale?

At the whale weigh station.

Where are most fish found?

Between the head and tail.

**How does an octopus
go to war?**
Well armed.

**What did the boy
octopus say to
the girl octopus?**
*I wanna hold your
hand, hand, hand,
hand, hand, hand,
hand, hand.*

**Have you heard about the
slippery eel?**
*I didn't think so. You wouldn't be
able to grasp it.*

**Did you hear about the fight
in the fish shop yesterday?**
Two fish got battered.

**Do dolphins do things
by accident?**
No. They do things on porpoise.

Do fish go on vacation?
No, they are always in schools.

How much does a crap eat?
Just a pinch.

**Why did the shark take so long
to eat the victim's arm?**
*Because the victim's watch made it
time consuming.*

**What's an eels
favorite song?**
Slip Sliding Away.

Animal Crackers

A mother and her son had just come home from the grocery store. Her son pulled out the box of animal crackers he begged her for and began spreading the animal shapes out on the table.

"What are you doing?" his mother asked.

"The box says you can't eat them if the seal is broken," the boy explained. "I'm looking for the seal."

King of the Jungle

Three animals were having a huge fight over who was the king of the jungle.

First, the hawk said because of his ability to fly, he could attack any prey repeatedly.

Second, the lion said he should be king because of his strength. No animal in the forest dared to challenge him.

Third, the skunk, insisted he didn't need flight nor strength to frighten off any animal. He would simply use his odor.

As the three animals argued, a grizzly bear came along and swallowed them all: hawk, lion, and stinker!

How can you tell a brown bear from a grizzly bear?

Climb a tree. If the bear climbs it and eats you, it's a brown bear. If the bear knocks the tree down and eats you, it's a grizzly bear.

What do you get if you cross an elephant with a whale?

A submarine with a built-in snorkel.

Why do elephants have trunks?

They'd look silly with glove compartments.

What kind of dog would be best to change a light bulb?

Golden Retriever: The sun is shining. We've got our whole day ahead of us. And you're worried about a stupid, burned out light bulb?

Dachshund: I can't reach it!

Poodle: I'll just talk sweet to the Lab. He'll do it, and while we're waiting my nails will dry.

Rottweiler: Go ahead! Make me!

Labrador Retriever: Oh, me, me!! Pleeeeze let me change the lightbulb! Can I? Can I? Huh? Huh? Can I?

Bloodhound: ZZZZZZZZZZZZ

Doberman Pinscher: While it's dark, I'm going to sleep on the couch.

Chihuahua: Yo quiero Taco Bulb?

Greyhound: It isn't moving. Who cares?

Old English Sheep Dog: Light bulb? That thing I just ate was a light bulb?

What does a cat think about?

1. Was that the can opener?
2. Why do humans make those noises with their mouth?
3. Who is going to do something about these stupid dogs?
4. Do you think those cats on TV really like that cat food?
5. Hmmm...If dogs serve humans, and humans serve cats, doesn't it make sense that dogs should serve cats?
6. This looks like a good spot for a nap.
7. If that really was the can opener, I'll play finicky just to let them know who's boss.

The Three Little Pigs

One day a first grade teacher was reading the story of the *Three Little Pigs* to her class. She came to the part of the story where the first pig was trying to gather the material for his home. She read, "...and so the pig went up to the man with the basket full of straw and said, 'Pardon me sir, but may I have some of that straw to build my house?'"

The teacher paused then asked the class, "And what do you think the man said?"

One little boy raised his hand and said, "I know...the man said, 'Holy cow! A talking pig!'"

Dog breeds that just didn't make it!

Collie + Lhasa Apso = Collapso, a dog that folds up for easy transport.

Collie + Malamute = Commute, a dog that travels to work.

Pekingese + Lhasa Apso = Peekasso, a dog that paints abstract.

Bloodhound + Labrador = Blabador, a dog that barks incessantly.

Malamute + Pointer = Moot Point, a dog that...oh nevermind, it doesn't matter.

Deerhound + Terrier = Derriere, a dog that's loyal to the end!